Yan Dehua's Bagua Applications
Chinese-English Edition

閻德華的八卦使用法

【少林破牆】

漢英對照版

a translation from the Chinese

by Andrea Mary Falk

霍安娣翻譯者

Canadian Cataloguing in Publication Data (original English
translation book)

Yen, Te-hua.

Yan Dehua's Bagua applications.

Translation of: Baguazhang shiyongfa.

1. Hand-to-hand fighting, Oriental. I. Falk, Andrea, 1954 - II. Title.
III. Title: Bagua applications.

GV1112.Y46 2000   796.815'5   C00-910889-0

The translation is of "*Baguazhang shiyongfa*" by Yan Dehua, 1936.
The diagrams are from "*Baguazhang shiyongfa*.". Published in
Chinese by Unicorn Press, Hong Kong. The book was also called
"*Shaolin Poqiang*".

The applications shown in this book are performed by
experienced martial artists. The author, translator and publishers
are not responsible for any injury that may occur while trying out
these techniques. Do not apply these techniques on anyone
without their consent and cooperation.

TABLE OF CONTENTS

Author's Preface

武技者操練身體之道技雖小而道理無窮凡
習拳術者須當練精化氣以氣化神以連使內
氣為功以川流不息為旨用求後天補先天之
法練功時以鼻孔引入清氣直入氣海由氣海
透過尾閭旋於腰間蓋兩腎之位在於腰實為
先天之第一要尤為諸臟之根源于是則腎水
足矣然後上升瞽脉而至丸宮仍歸鼻間以舌
接引腎氣而下則下腹充實漸入丹田此即週
天至要義

When martial artists train their bodies, although there are not that many techniques, the principles behind them are inexhaustible. Those who train martial arts must refine their essence to transform their energy/power [qì], in order for this energy to transform their spirit. They view mastery as the ability to use this internal energy and hold as a goal its constant flow without impediment, so seek out techniques that enable their acquired *qi* to supplement their original *qi*. The storage of the original *qi* is of primary importance, and enables the kidney fluid to be sufficient. To train this, breathe the pure air in through the nose and take it straight to the belly. From the belly, it absorbs into the tailbone then turns in the midriff to store in the kidneys, which are in the body core. Then it goes up the Governing Vessel to the brain and returns through the nasal passage to connect by the tongue, which draws the kidney *qi* so that it descends. When it descends to the abdomen it solidifies and enters the cinnabar field. This is the requirement for a complete cycle.

諸般拳術皆以內氣為主以外勁為功練功之要義在於日必操習永無間斷而氣
質充盈古人云天得以清地得以寧人得以靈久練之則得天地之靈機自然之活
潑誠於中而形於外伸縮敏捷剛柔相濟進退合法緩急得宜術中奧妙則自然得
之矣

All martial arts regard internal energy as the root and outer power as proficiency. To train to be accomplished you must train every day over a long period without a break so that your *qi* becomes full. The ancients said, "When heaven (the head) becomes clear and the earth (body) becomes serene, then man has one spirit." Those who train for a long time gain the ingenious spirit of heaven and earth – they are naturally agile, they are completely centered and this shows in their form. They can extend and contract agilely, use a perfect balance of hard and soft, enter and withdraw as needed, be as unhurried or quick as they desire. The perfect subtleties of their techniques are all naturally acquired.

鄙人自幼年時喜拳勇愛武技因投周祥師之門練習八卦掌乃得嫡係之真傳而練藝一道雖得名師乃習在各人余平生所習者不遇平常之技今著八掌使用法詳細圖解三百六十手是尊從前人苦心精詣遺留之術誠恐久而淹沒故且步其後塵以達後學者不失真傳而已矣

I loved martial arts since I was young, so I learned from master Zhou Xiang. As an apprentice, I learned the true tradition of Baguazhang with morals. Although I learned from a famous master, training is the result of personal work, so my skills are not above ordinary. Now I have written "Baguazhang Applications" with its three hundred and sixty (*sic*) detailed drawings to set down the hard won knowledge of past generations before it is lost. I wrote this book so that the true skills are not lost to future generations.

鄙人之見不以門戶派別而分以公開鑒賞為本旨望各界愛好武術者注意參考乃我之幸也

It is my pleasure to present this book openly to those who love martial arts wherever they are, and whatever style they do.

丙子年三月　日

河北省武清縣閻德華謹序

Yan Dehua

Wuqing county, Hebei province

March 1936

Translator's Preface

For years I've enjoyed these little shape-changing men with their expressive faces and hands. I am glad to have finally translated this book with the same hope as Master Yan – to hand on the tradition and bring enjoyment to those who care about the martial arts.

This book shows how people can play Baguazhang with love and respect for their tradition and their sparring partner. This is pure Baguazhang – nothing more needs to be said. For this reason, I have not edited or made any commentary at all, and kept the flavour of the original book as much as possible.

Any mistakes remaining in the text are my responsibility alone. I apologize for the fact that a translation is never as good as the original, even more so than usual, because Master Yan's writing was as individualist as his drawings.

Andrea Mary Falk, 霍安娣

Victoria, Canada

August 2000

Editor's Preface to the Chinese-English Edition

I enjoy this little book so much that I just had to do a Chinese-English edition when the book's latest print run ran out. I particularly like the surprised look on the face of Yan's partner every single time he loses the exchange.

I changed a bit of my original translation, because I just couldn't help myself. Some new errors have certainly crept in, as typing in Chinese is fraught with possibilities for error.

Andrea Mary Falk, 霍安娣

Québec, Canada

May 2019

Preface to the 20th Anniversary hard cover editions

At this 20th anniversary of the establishment of tgl books, I have finally completed the reworking of all the books to be available for print to order. To celebrate, I have made hard cover copies of all the translations – the Li Tianji, Jiang Rongqiao, and Di Guoyong books, as well as this one. In setting up the hard cover editions, I of course made a few minor changes, but the translations are all in their final state now. If there are any remaining mistakes, that is just too bad.

Andrea Mary Falk

霍安娣

Québec, Canada

February, 2021

第一手名為撞掌

The first method is called Shove with the Palm [zhuàng zhǎng]

敵來右掌擊我上部我速坐身出右掌掩截其臂

My opponent strikes towards my head with his right palm. I quickly sit back and extend my right palm to intercept his arm, tucking in my elbow [yǎn jié].

再速用左手由我右臂下穿出而顧其右臂

I then quickly thread [chuān] my left hand under my
right arm to deal with his right arm.

THE FIRST METHOD

敵必用左掌再擊而我復用右手搨其胸而同時進身

My opponent has no option but to use his left hand to strike again, so I enter with my body and use my right hand again to firmly tamp on [tà] his chest.

敵必卸而掌擊來我再以右手向其左肩間穿去

My opponent has no option but to unload and strike
again, so I use my right hand again to thread [chuān]
onto his left shoulder joint.

再反手擄其肘同時撤左掌

Then I roll my hand over to pull [lǚ] his elbow while removing my left hand.

而右手往上托再坐身形

I lift from underneath [tuō] with my right hand and settle into my legs.

THE FIRST METHOD

腰用力而鬆右手以左掌擊其肋敵當敗矣

I snap force from my body core to my right hand and hit [jī] my opponent's ribs with my left hand and he is defeated.

本招為甲乙丙丁戊己庚七圖黑褲者即我花褲者為敵
In the seven drawings of this exchange I am in black trousers and my opponent is in patterned trousers.

第二手名為掖掌

The second method is called Steal in the Palm [yē zhǎng]

此法是由我向敵以右掌擊去敵速吸胸而往右拗身

In this method, I attack my opponent with a right palm strike. He quickly sucks in his chest [xī xiōng] and turns sideways to put his right side forward.

再用右手攦我腕左手托我肘

My opponent then pulls [lǚ] my wrist with his right hand and lifts [tuō] my elbow from underneath with his left hand.

而我速將右手極力向我左側

I quickly, and with maximum force, drive my right
hand to my left side.

上穿以卸敵之手之力

I thread my hand up [shàng chuān] to dissipate the

force of my opponent's double grip.

遂再往下捂肘即掩肘式掩至我肘對我左肋時手心相
對敵之右肋而我左手顧其右臂

I then continue on down, 'swallowing' my elbow to
tuck it in to form a cover elbow posture [yǎn zhǒu].
When my elbow is tucked in beside my left ribs, my
palm is opposite my opponent's right ribs and my left
hand deals with [gù] his right arm.

同時提右腿

At this time, I lift my right leg.

全身之力皆貫於兩掌再落右步

I put the power of my whole body into my two hands
and land the right foot.

THE SECOND METHOD

鬆肩打之

I hit him with a release through the shoulders.

本招為甲乙丙丁戊己庚辛八圖黑褲者即我花褲者為
敵請注意焉 Please take note that in the eight
drawings of this exchange I am in black trousers and
my opponent is in patterned trousers.

第三手名白猿搬枝

The third method is called White Ape Removes a Branch [bái yuán bān zhī]

我用右掌擊敵胸敵速吸胸

I strike at my opponent's chest with my right hand.

He quickly sucks in his chest [xī xiōng].

右手扣擄我之右腕而左手擄我肘環

My opponent grabs and pulls [kòu lǚ] my right wrist
with his right hand and pulls [lǚ] my elbow joint with
his left hand.

我速將右手往下插

I quickly stab [chā] my right hand down.

THE THIRD METHOD

寧轉向外

I twist [nǐng] my arm to the outside.

而往上反同時上扣左步下身形再以左手托其臂起右
腿

And turn my hand over to face up. At the same time,
I advance my left foot, hooking in, and drop my
weight down. I then lift [tuō] his arm with my left
hand and raise my right foot.

轉身搶其位敵之右臂肘恰在左檢頭

I turn to steal his place. My opponent's right elbow is
now conveniently on my left shoulder.

再用左手附之其腕腰間用力敵必過我頭由後向前僕
倒

I use my left hand to move his wrist and use the
power of my body core. He must fly over my head
from behind me to fall in front of me.

本招為甲乙丙丁戊己庚七圖黑褲者即我花褲者為敵
請注意焉 Please take note that in the seven drawings
of this exchange I am in black trousers and my
opponent is in patterned trousers.

第四手名綑身大纏

The fourth method is called Coil Around the Body to Bind it [kǔn shēn dà chǎn]

敵右拳打來速吸身卸之用右手攄其腕敵力解

My opponent punches with his right fist. I quickly absorb with my body [xī shēn] to evade the punch, and pull his wrist with my right hand to dissipate his force.

我速震右腳上左步搶其位而我左步吃其右腿同時以
左臂肘猛力挎敵臂敵臂必曲

I quickly stamp my right foot and step my left foot forward to take his place [qiǎng], controlling [chī 'eat'] his right leg with my left leg. At the same time, I strongly catch my elbow into his arm so that he has to bend his arm.

我左手由其臂掖下向其後背穿去以左指扣其左肋往
後掰此時右手高揚過頂（或當胸護門或擊其面而防
敵之左手為是）

I sneak my left hand under his armpit and around his
back so that it threads through to tuck onto his left
ribs. I can then pull to the rear to toss him. As I do
this I lift my right hand above my head, ready to
protect my chest, hit his face, or block a possible
strike from his left hand.

本招三圖為甲乙丙每圖二人黑褲者即此灰褲者為彼
請注意焉 Please take note that in each of the three drawings of
this exchange I am in black trousers and the other party is in grey
trousers.

第五手名為截腿

The fifth method is called Leg Interception [jié tuǐ]

我以右掌擊敵而敵用右手擄扣我腕左手托我肘環向
下彈之我必前僕

I strike at my opponent with my right hand. He grabs and pulls [lǔ kòu] my wrist with his right hand and lifts [tuō] my elbow up with his left hand. He changes this to a downward snap [tán] to make me fall forward.

而速出左腿向前橫截其右腿

I quickly put my left foot forward (turned out, to

cross with his leg) to intercept [héng jié] his right leg.

敵必將右步提起我足落空而我速出左手由我嘴角間
發出戳其目

My opponent must lift his right leg. My foot will then
miss and land on the ground and I can quickly dart
out my left hand from my jaw to poke [chuō] at his
eyes.

敵必棄我右臂而變招我速進身形上右步吃其步買其
腰而用右臂橫其胸臂向外滾同時塌肩頂項變臉目視
敵面五行合一取開勁敵必後僕

My opponent must release my right arm and change his tactic. I quickly move in, stepping my right leg in to get my body in close, control [chī 'eat'] his legs, and control [mǎi 'buy'] his waist. I place my right arm horizontally across his chest and arm to roll him out. As I do this, I settle my shoulders, straighten my neck, and change my face to look at my opponent's face. The five elements combine within me to create an opening power and my opponent must fall behind me.

本招四圖為甲乙丙丁每圖二人黑褲者即此灰褲者為彼請
注意焉 Please take note that in each of the four drawings of this exchange I am in black trousers and the other party is in grey trousers.

第六手名為巧倒銀瓶

The sixth method is called Cleverly Knock Over the Silver Vase [qiǎo dǎo yín píng]

與敵相較之站向為順步先左手在上右手在下兩手心右沖
上左沖下（此式為獅子大張嘴）二目注視敵之兩肩（腳
踢膀歪拳打膀斜）敵若以右腿踢我我速以右手向下插
（下立椿）遂提右腿

Facing off against my opponent in the same stance [shùn bù, same arm and leg forward], I place my left hand up with the palm facing down and my right hand down with the palm facing up. This is called Lion Opens Its Mouth Wide [shīzǐ dà zhāng zuǐ]. I watch my opponent's shoulders. If he is going to kick, his shoulders will tilt [wāi]; if he is going to punch, his shoulders will twist [xié]. If he kicks at me with his right foot I quickly stab my right hand down to lift his leg.

再將右手向上纏其腿取黏勁速落右步而上左步吃其
左步再以左掌擊其腹敵必僕

I then lift my right hand to encircle his leg, and, using
sticking power I quickly land my right foot and step
in my left to take over [chī 'eat'] his left leg. I also hit
his abdomen with my left palm so he must fall down.

本招為甲乙二圖每圖二人黑褲者即此灰褲者為彼請
注意焉 Please take note that in each of the two
drawings of this exchange I am in black trousers and
the other party is in grey trousers.

第七手名為雙換掌

The seventh method is called Double Changeover Palm [shuāng huàn zhǎng]

敵以左掌擊我面我遂以右腕掩其臂

My opponent strikes at my face with his left hand. I tuck in to cover [yǎn] his arm with my right wrist.

左手由我右臂下敵之臂外向上穿而同時上左步以左
臂黏其臂

I thread my left hand under my right arm to thread it along and up, sticking to the outside of my opponent's arm. At the same time, I step my left foot forward so that my left arm controls his arm.

同時再以右掌擊其左肋

At the same time, I use my right hand again to hit [jī]

his ribs

THE SEVENTH METHOD

敵當擰步進身卸我右掌而速抽左掌再出右掌擊我左
肋我速吸身再將左臂往下由敵之右臂裏黏棚其臂

My opponent twists his stance to enter his body and
dissipate the attack of my right hand. He quickly
pulls his left hand away then hits to my left ribs with
his right hand. I quickly absorb with my body [xī
shēn] then roll my left arm down and out, sticking to
his right arm to press it [péng] outwards.

再下身形以左臂纏敵之右臂我頭由敵腕下過我左臂
往裏抱

I then drop down further and wrap my left arm
around [chán] his right arm. My head ducks under his
wrist so that my left arm can come back to wrap
inward.

而同時再將右手由我左臂下向上穿貼其臂

At the same time, I thread my right hand up under
my left arm to stick on [tiē] his arm.

同時再以左掌擊敵右肋敵必敗招

At the same time, I use my left hand again to hit his right ribs. My opponent must lose this exchange.

本招為甲乙丙丁戊己庚七圖黑褲者即我花褲者為敵請注意焉 Please take note that in each of the seven drawings of this exchange I am in black trousers and my opponent is in patterned trousers.

第八手名為回身突撞

The eighth method is called Turn Around and Suddenly Shove [huí shēn tū zhuàng]

我用左拳擊敵前胸敵必向右吸身而以左手向外吃我
腕而以右掌擊我肩

I punch to my opponent's chest with my left fist. He must absorb with his body [xī shēn] to the right, control my wrist outwards with his left hand, and strike my shoulder with his right hand.

而我速向回轉身

I quickly turn my body around to the back.

THE EIGHTH METHOD

震左腿而起右步

I stamp my left foot and lift my right leg.

再用左手扶右腕小臂與肩平而虛右步

I use my left hand to support [fú] my right wrist and

forearm at shoulder height and empty my right leg.

THE EIGHTH METHOD

再往下滾肘落右步坐身形塌肩甲長腰身以小臂橫撞
其右肋敵必傾倒

I then roll my elbows downward, set my right leg
down, sit down, settle my shoulder blades, and
lengthen my back in order to use my forearm to
shove with my arm across [héng zhuàng] his right
ribs. My opponent must fall back.

本招為甲乙丙丁戊五圖黑褲者即我花褲者為敵請注
意焉 Please take note that in each of the five
drawings of this exchange I am in black trousers and
my opponent is in patterned trousers.

第九手名為左右坡腿

The ninth method is called Left and Right Sloping Kicks [zuǒ yòu pō tuǐ]

敵用右拳擊我胸我速向左吸身而虛右步再以右手由
敵臂下擄敵腕

My opponent punches to my chest with his right fist.
I quickly absorb with my body [xī shēn] back to the
left and sit onto the left leg, emptying the right leg. I
use my right hand to pull his wrist down.

再速震掰右步

I quickly stamp my right foot, opening it out [zhèn bāi].

再以左腿踢其右步同時以左手由敵臂裏往下插而外開

I then kick my opponent's right leg with my left leg, stab down my left hand inside his arm and open out [wài kāi].

THE NINTH METHOD

敵必抽由手而出左拳起右腿卸我左腿

My opponent must pull his right hand away [chōu],

punch with his left fist, and lift his right leg to evade

my left leg.

我速震掰左步而用左手擄敵左腕

I quickly stamp my left foot, opened out [zhèn bāi],

and pull [lǚ] his left wrist with my left hand.

THE NINTH METHOD

同時起右腿踢敵右步而右手由敵左臂裏往下插而向
外開重量載於左步拗項回頭目視敵面而起左手敵必
敗

I lift my right leg and kick [tī] my opponent's right leg.
I stab my right hand down inside his left arm and
open up [wài kāi]. I plant my weight on my left leg,
turn my head to look at my opponent and lift my left
hand. My opponent must lose this exchange.

本招為甲乙丙丁戊已六圖黑褲者即我花褲者為敵請
注意焉 Please take note that in each of the six
drawings of this exchange I am in black trousers and
my opponent is in patterned trousers.

第十掌名為巧挎花籃

The tenth method is called Cleverly Carry the Flower Basket Over Your Arm [qiǎo kuà huā lán]

敵用右掌擊我前胸我速吸化

My opponent strikes to my chest with his right hand.

I quickly evade [xī huà].

再用左手扣其腕而以右肘剋其臂

I use my left hand to tuck onto [kòu] his wrist and my

right elbow to restrain [kè] his arm.

同時上左步再用右指戳其目

At the same time, I step my left foot forward and stab
my right fingers at [chuō] his eyes.

THE TENTH METHOD

敵必用左掌擊我面我速以右臂向上滾肘

My opponent must strike at my face with his left
hand. I quickly roll the elbow of my right arm up [gǔn
zhǒu].

而用左掌擊敵右肩須坐身形

I hit my opponent's right shoulder with my left hand.

I must settle my body down [zuò shēn] to do this.

THE TENTH METHOD

兩手用榨力敵必仰倒

I apply a force that spreads all my fingers [zhā lì] and
my opponent must fall back.

本招為甲乙丙丁戊已六圖黑褲者即我花褲者為敵請
注意焉 Please take note that in each of the six
drawings of this exchange I am in black trousers and
my opponent is in patterned trousers.

第十一手名為搜肚掌

The eleventh method is called Search the Belly Palm [sōu dù zhǎng]

我以右掌擊敵胸

I strike at my opponent's chest with my right hand.

敵必卸而攦我右腕又以左掌打我面

My opponent has to dissipate my attack by pulling [lǚ] my right wrist. He then hits to my face with his left hand.

而我速向右擰身而卸之再掰右步提左腿

I quickly twist my body [níng shēn] to the right to
dissipate his attack, open my right foot out, and lift
my left leg.

THE ELEVENTH METHOD

進身形而同時右手向外掰而左臂由敵左臂外往下插
而左腿自我右腿上過仍落原處捬項回頭目視敵而右
掌上穿左掌打其襠

I enter my body while rotating and opening my right hand outward and stabbing my left arm down outside my opponent's left arm. I step my left leg across my right, back to where it was, turning my neck to look back at my opponent. I thread my right palm up and strike my opponent's groin with my left palm.

敵當封閉而卸之遂撲擊於我而我再撤右腿而虛之曲
左腿下身形而轉身再左手出於右肩頭而右手備於左
胯下取勾子手而左手防敵手

My opponent closes down [fēng bì] and evades my
attack, and strikes at my face. I pull back my right leg
again – keeping my weight off it – crouch down low
with my weight on my left leg, and turn. I put my left
hand up by my right shoulder and head. My right
hand prepares to strike by forming a hook down by
the left hip as my left hand blocks the attack.

敵來我再上右步以右手腕反打其襠敵必敗

As my opponent comes in, I advance my right foot to bring the back of my right wrist to hit his groin. My opponent must lose this exchange.

本招為甲乙丙丁戊已六圖黑褲者即我花褲者為敵請注意焉 Please take note that in each of the six drawings of this exchange I am in black trousers and my opponent is in patterned trousers.

第十二手名為太公釣魚

The twelfth method is called Great-grandfather Goes Fishing [tài gōng diào yú]

敵用右拳擊我而我速以右臂掩其臂

My opponent punches me with his right fist. I quickly tuck my right arm [yǎn] onto his right arm.

而同時扣其右步轉身形而提左腿再將左手由左肋下
向背後插

At the same time, I hook my right foot in and turn my
body around as I lift my left leg. I stab [chā] my left
hand down along my left ribs behind my back.

再速落左步左手自敵胸前穿去面右手搬捏其喉或戳
其目

I quickly land my left foot and thread my left hand out along my opponent's chest. With my right hand I can either twist [bān niē] his throat or stab [chuō] his eyes.

THE TWELFTH METHOD

遂再以左臂由左向右攤力往下切而敵必仰倒

I can then throw by cutting my left arm around from left to right with a downwards spreading power [tān lì] and my opponent must fall down on his back.

本招為甲乙丙丁四圖黑褲者即我花褲者為敵請注意焉 Please take note that in each of the four drawings of this exchange I am in black trousers and my opponent is in patterned trousers.

[Translator's note: The name of this move refers to fish rising to old Jiang Ziya's line, which is hookless and baitless – so refers to a willing victim putting its own head in the noose, to mix a metaphor.]

第十三手名為活步撩陰砲

The thirteenth method is called Tease the Hidden Cannon on the Move [huó bù liāo yǐn pào]

敵用右掌擊我面我遂以右臂掩其臂而再用右拳沖敵面

My opponent strikes at my face with his right hand. I tuck my right arm around his arm [yǎn] and carry on to punch [chōng] his face with my right fist.

敵必卸我速將拳由自胸前往下反變掌撩其襠

He must evade the strike, so I quickly switch from in front of his chest, opening my hand and turning my palm over to slice up [liāo] to his groin.

而同時將右腿提掰上半步速出左拳沖其面而上左步

At the same time, I lift and advance my right foot a half step, opened out, and quickly step my left foot forward and punch [chōng] his face with my left hand.

敵又封卸之我速將左拳由自胸前往下反變掌撩其襠

My opponent closes off and dissipates [fēng xiè] my

attack again. I quickly bring my left fist from in front

of his chest, open it, and turn it over to slice up [liāo]

to his groin

敵當卸閉而退右步我速將左手往上撩而同時將左腿
提掰上半步再速進身上右步再同時出右拳沖打其面
敵必敗

My opponent dissipates and shuts down [xiè bì] my attack and steps his right leg back. I quickly slice [liāo] my left hand up, advance my left leg a half step, opening out, and advance a full step with my right to enter with my body. At the same time, I punch my right fist to his face. My opponent must lose this exchange.

本招為甲乙丙丁戊五圖黑褲者即我花褲者為敵請注
意焉 Please take note that in each of the five drawings of this exchange I am in black trousers and my opponent is in patterned trousers.

第十四手名為倒提金爐

The fourteenth method is called Lift and Pour the Golden Brazier [dào tí jīn lú]

敵用右掌劈面打來我速坐身以右手往上穿

My opponent comes at me with a right chop [pī] to my face. I quickly sit back and thread my right hand up.

而同時再用左手擄其肘環速上扣左步踏扣其襠

At the same time, I grab his elbow and pull [lǚ] with my left hand and quickly step my left foot with the foot hooked in to pressure [tā kòu] his groin.

遂轉身形再右手向後搬其臀而帶襠

I turn my body and extend my right hand to carry [bān] his buttocks and take [dài] his groin on my back.

由後往前以膀肩及腰間用力而付身形再以臀步擊其
腹敵必前僕

I bend over [fú shēn] and use the power of my upper arms and shoulders together with that of my body core to throw from behind me towards the front, while also striking his abdomen with my hip. My opponent must fall forward.

本招為甲乙丙丁四圖黑褲者即我條褲者為敵請注意
焉 Please take note that in each of the four drawings of this exchange I am in black trousers and my opponent is in striped trousers.

第十五手名為滾臂捶

The fifteenth method is called Roll the Arms and Thump [gǔn bèi chuí]

敵用左拳擊我胸我速以右臂掩其臂

My opponent punches to my chest with his left fist. I quickly tuck my right arm [yǎn] onto his arm.

同時向右側閃身手與肩平以我臂貼其臂面往裏抱遂
由左側向後偷倒在左步

At the same time, I dodge my body [shǎn shēn] to the right, and, with my hand at shoulder height, keep my arm stuck [tiē] onto his arm. I roll in to keep control and steal my left foot behind through on the left.

再往下滾肘以反背捶擊其腹或襠

I roll my elbow further over [gǔn zhǒu] to roll my fist over to thump [chuí jī] his abdomen or groin with a backfist.

而再往後兩臂用力開之遂長身形敵必仰倒

I then lengthen my body [cháng shēn] and open my
arms out with force, and my opponent must fall over
on his back.

本招為甲乙丙丁四圖黑褲者即我花褲者為敵請注意
焉 Please take note that in each of the four drawings
of this exchange I am in black trousers and my
opponent is in patterned trousers.

第十六手名為抽身點肋

The sixteenth method is called Draw Out the Body to Poke the Ribs [chōu shēn diǎn lèi]

敵來右拳擊我胸我向右扭身

My opponent comes at me with a right punch to my chest. I twist my body [niǔ shēn] to the right.

遂上左步而同時右手由其臂下橫穿復擄扣其腕

I step my left foot forward and thread my right hand along under his arm (palm across his arm) [héng chuān] to trap and grab [lü kòu] his wrist.

敵必抗而隨其力向上提其腕

My opponent must resist this [kàng], so I follow his force to lift his wrist up in the direction he pulls.

而速以左手四指點其肋步眼不動兩足尖用力擰身而
進之

I then quickly stab the four fingers of my left hand into his ribs. I do not move my foot or head (eyes) position, but twist my body [níng shēn] and enter by driving force from my feet – pivoting on the balls of my feet.

本招為甲乙丙丁四圖黑褲者即我條褲者為敵請注意
焉 Please take note that in each of the four drawings of this exchange I am in black trousers and my opponent is in striped trousers.

THE SIXTEENTH METHOD

第十七手名為金鉤掛環

The seventeenth method is called Golden Hook Hooks the Ring [jīn gōu guà huán]

敵來右拳擊我面門我速用左手掩其臂而右手由我左腕下敵之右臂外向上穿

My opponent comes at me to punch my face with his right fist. I quickly tuck onto [yǎn] his arm with my left hand and bring my right hand under my left wrist to thread up outside his right arm.

同時上左步而右手由上往下擄其腕

At the same time, I step my left foot forward and pull
his wrist down with my right hand.

THE SEVENTEENTH METHOD

再已左拳反貫其而敵必卸我目注視敵肩

I then turn my left fist over to do a hooking punch [fǎn guàn] to his ear. He must evade my attack. I watch his shoulders carefully.

如敵肩稍動我遂起右腿橫其右步而同時右手往下擄
重量載於左步擰身甩臉目視敵面敵必敗

If he moves his shoulders at all, I quickly lift my right
leg to sweep [héng] his right leg and pull down [xià
lǚ] with my right hand. I plant my weight strongly on
my left leg, twist my body, and turn my head to look
at his face. My opponent must lose this exchange.

本招為甲乙丙丁四圖黑褲者即我條褲者為敵請注意
焉 Please take note that in each of the four drawings
of this exchange I am in black trousers and my
opponent is in striped trousers.

第十八手名為金雞抖翎

The eighteenth method is called Golden Pheasant Shakes its Wings [jīn jī dǒu líng]

我與敵人過招時或又來第二者自左側以右手將我脖
項按住

During an exchange with my opponent, or if a second opponent comes from behind, I find myself with my opponent on my left, pushing down [àn zhù] my neck with his right hand.

我速下身形往下低頭

I quickly drop down [xià shēn] and lower my head.

THE EIGHTEENTH METHOD

而將左肩往下塌再由敵之右腕下往上反

I sink [xià tā] my left shoulder then roll it up [shàng

fǎn] under my opponent's right wrist.

而以肩打其腕敵腕必開

Then I hit his wrist with my shoulder. My opponent
must release his grip.

窩再速以左手打其襠敵必張倒

I then quickly strike his groin with my left hand. My opponent must open up and fall down.

本招為甲乙丙丁戊五圖黑褲者即我灰褲者為敵請注意焉 Please take note that in each of the four drawings of this exchange I am in black trousers and my opponent is in grey trousers.

第十九手名為雙抱掌

The nineteenth method is called Embrace in both Hands [shuāng bào zhǎng]

敵以右掌擊我胸我速以左手掩其腕右掌由自左臂下
敵之右臂上穿出

My opponent strikes at my chest with his right hand. I quickly cover [yǎn] his wrist with my left hand and bring my right hand under my left arm to thread out over his right arm.

而反攤其力遂坐身形兩掌大指皆朝上而相隔三四寸

兩臂齊併兩肘皆往裏抱緊靠

I open and spread out to reverse his force. I sit down
and place my hands about three to four inches apart
with the fingers pointing up, the arms together, and
the elbows rolled in tightly.

而兩掌左顧其臂右對其肋向上挫擊之而敵必敗招

My left hand deals with his arm and my right goes for his ribs as I strike sharply upwards [cuò jī]. My opponent must lose this exchange.

本招為甲乙丙三圖黑褲者即我灰褲者為敵請注意焉
Please take note that in each of the four drawings of this exchange I am in black trousers and my opponent is in grey trousers.

第二十手名為金蟬脫殼

The twentieth method is called Golden Cicada Sloughs its Skin [jīn chán tuō kē]

敵以右掌擊我上部我速以右手向上穿

My opponent strikes high with his right hand. I quickly thread my right hand up [shàng chuān].

而擄其腕敵必挺勁再遂向上提

I pull his wrist. My opponent must straighten himself up [tǐng jìn] to raise his hand.

速上扣左腿

I quickly lift my left foot, tucked in.

以胯貼其腹再用左手反打其襠

I stick my hip in tight [tiē] to his abdomen and turn

my left hand over to strike [fǎn dǎ] his groin.

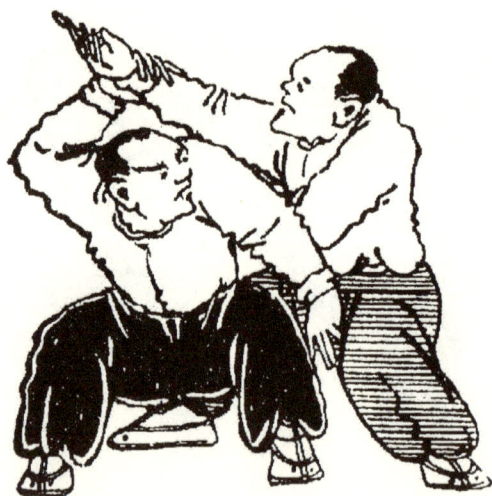

THE TWENTIETH METHOD

同時再向前斜肩伏身形腰間用力而目視左手擊之

At the same time, I also tilt my shoulders [xié jiān] and lean forward [fú shēn], using power from my body core as I look at my left hand's strike.

敵必前僕

My opponent must dive forward.

本招為甲乙丙丁戊已六圖黑褲者即我灰褲者為敵請
注意 Please take note that in each of the six drawings
of this exchange I am in black trousers and my
opponent is in grey trousers.

第二十一手名為摘捶勒打

The twenty-first method is called Pluck, Pound, Restrain and Hit [zhāi chuí lèi dǎ]

我以右掌擊敵而敵必吸胸卸之

I hit at my opponent with my right hand. He must suck in his chest [xī xiōng] to dissipate my attack.

而同時以右手擄我右腕左手必托我肘

At the same time, he pulls my right wrist with his
right hand and lifts [tuō] my elbow with his left hand.

THE TWENTY-FIRST METHOD

我速將右手由下往上反（小之反上）向上斜穿同時
上左步以左手由我右臂下出而擄敵之左手

I quickly turn my right hand over (I twist my little
finger up) [fǎn] and thread it diagonally upward
while advancing my left foot. I thread my left hand
out under my right arm to pull on my opponent's left
hand.

速吞右臂進身形遂上右步吃其右腿

I quickly draw in my right arm and enter my whole body, stepping my right foot forward to take over [chī 'eat'] his right leg.

THE TWENTY-FIRST METHOD

而再扣襠撐步坐身形開左手以右臂橫其腹一力擊之

I then tuck in my groin, twist my stance and settle down [zuò shēn] while I open my left hand and sweep [héng] my right arm across his abdomen. These forces work all together.

本招為甲乙丙丁戊五圖黑褲者即我灰褲者為敵請注意焉 Please take note that in each of the five drawings of this exchange I am in black trousers and my opponent is in grey trousers.

第二十二手名為倒揹金人

The twenty-second method is called Carry a Barbarian Over Your Back [dǎo bēi jīn rén]

敵用雙手扣擄我之雙腕

My opponent uses both hands to lock onto and pull [kòu lǔ] both my wrists.

我速將兩手左向右右向左在自己胸前橫穿

I quickly thread my hands across each other [héng chuān] in front of my chest – my left hand moving right and my right hand moving left.

由下往上反而兩手再擄敵之兩腕向懷中領

I turn my hands over and up from below [fǎn], then pull my opponent's wrists to draw them into my chest.

THE TWENTY-SECOND METHOD

速將敵之左臂掖在敵之右臂折窩下再往敵之右腿外
上扣右步

I quickly tuck [yē] my opponent's left arm under his
right armpit, then step my right foot forward, hooked
in, outside his right leg.

同時進轉身形以右手顧其左腕以左手顧其右臂速下
身形取跪膝再用雙手攀其右腕而以右肩擔之

At the same time, I enter and turn my body. My right
hand takes care of his left wrist and my left hand
takes care of his right arm. I quickly drop my body
[xià shēn] and kneel, then use both hands to drag
down [pān] his right wrist so that I support his arm
on my right shoulder.

同時腰間用力以臂股拱其腹挺項甩臉取合一勁由後
往前揹之敵必張過

At the same time, I drive force from my body core
and drive my buttocks into his abdomen. I hold my
neck up and throw my head – all forces uniting as one
[hé yī jìn] – so that I take him over my back. My
opponent must be stretched out and passed over me.

本招為甲乙丙丁戊己六圖黑褲者即我灰褲者為敵請
注意焉 Please take note that in each of the six
drawings of this exchange I am in black trousers and
my opponent is in grey trousers.

第二十三手名為聯珠簡

The twenty-third method is called Arrows like a String of Pearls [lián zhū jiàn]

此招又名繃拳三進我與敵相較我以右拳先擊其胸

This trick is also called Enter Three Times Continuously with Driving Punches [bēng quán sān jìn]. In an exchange with my opponent, I punch to his chest with my right fist.

敵欲勁而再以左拳繼之

My opponent moves to evade my punch, so I punch
again with my left fist.

敵欲化復仍以右拳擊之出手時須坐身重量載於後步
而前步虛之

My opponent prepares to counter attack, so I punch
once again with my right fist. When I punch, I must
sit down with my weight planted on my back leg and
keep my front leg empty.

本招為甲乙丙三圖黑褲者即我灰褲者為敵請注意焉
Please take note that in each of the three drawings of
this exchange I am in black trousers and my
opponent is in grey trousers.

第二十四手名為上步斜身雙掖掌

The twenty-fourth method is called Advance with an Angled Body to Steal in with Both Palms [shàng bù xié shēn shuāng yē zhǎng]

敵以右掌劈面打來

My opponent comes at me with a right chop [pī] to my face.

我速用右掌顧其臂外向上穿而手穿至其肘以上為適
宜而防其轉環手

I quickly thread [shàng chuān] my right hand up along
the outside of his arm – fingers aligned along the arm
– until my hand arrives above his elbow. From there
I can easily defend against his arm by simply
rotating.

我再以纏綿勁而勁不解速進身上左步同時再將右手
往下反以四指戳其右掖窩而我右肘仍防其肘

I use coiling power [chǎn mián jìn], without any break
in my power application, to quickly enter my body by
advancing my left foot. At the same time, I turn my
right hand over so that my fingers stab [chuō] into his
right armpit while my right elbow still defends
against his elbow.

同時再以左手用鷹捉力戳敵之右肋

At the same time, I use eagle clutching power to stab [chuō] his right ribs with my left hand.

THE TWENTY-FOURTH METHOD

速坐身形腰間用力以雙手合一勁送之敵必敗招

I quickly drop my body and drive force from my whole body core to push him away with a fully connected power through to both hands. My opponent must lose this exchange.

本招為甲乙丙丁戊五圖黑褲者即我灰褲者為敵請注意焉 Please take note that in each of the five drawings of this exchange I am in black trousers and my opponent is in grey trousers.

第二十五手名為協肩搜肚掌

The twenty-fifth method is called Combine the Shoulders to Search the Belly [xié jiān sōu dǔ zhǎng]

敵用右手擄我右腕

My opponent pulls on [lǚ] my right wrist with his right hand.

我速將右手往上反至小指沖上向我左肩間穿去敵手
必開我再往下扣擄敵腕而同時速往敵之右步後上左
步

I quickly turn over [fǎn] my right hand and drive the

little finger up to thread up [chuān] towards my left

shoulder. My opponent's hand must open. I then tuck

my hand over to grab and pull his wrist down while

quickly stepping my left foot in behind his right foot.

而用左肩擊打敵人之右肩同時再以左手反背打其腹
（不遇歹人萬別打其襠）敵必僕倒

I hit my opponent's right shoulder with my left shoulder. At the same time, I strike his abdomen with the back [fǎn bèi dǎ] of my left hand (do not by any means strike his groin unless he is a vicious enemy). My opponent must fall forward.

而用左肩擊打敵人之右肩

I use my left shoulder to strike [jī dǎ] my opponent's
right shoulder.

同時再以左手反背打其腹（不遇歹人萬別打其襠）
敵必僕倒

At the same time, I strike his abdomen with the back [fǎn bèi dǎ] of my left hand (do not by any means strike his groin if he is not a real enemy). My opponent must fall prostrate.

本招為甲乙丙丁戊五圖黑褲者即我灰褲者為敵請注意焉 Please take note that in each of the five drawings of this exchange I am in black trousers and my opponent is in grey trousers.

第二十六手名為回身削肋掌

The twenty-sixth method is called Turn Back and Slice the Ribs [huí shēn xiāo lèi zhǎng]

敵與我相較我以右掌擊敵中部

In an exchange with my opponent, I strike to his centre with my right palm.

敵必吸胸以卸之而用右手由我臂外向上穿復攎我腕

My opponent must suck in his chest [xī xiōng] to evade the attack. He threads his right hand up outside my arm then turns it to grab my wrist.

　　　　　　THE TWENTY-SIXTH METHOD

我稍動敵發掌必由我臂上擊我面部

I move slightly to cause my opponent's hand to slide
up along my arm to hit towards my face instead.

我速以左手由我口間向上出而指抓其右指

I quickly bring my left hand up past my mouth to grab [zhuā] the fingers of his right hand.

而急上左步縮頸藏頭同時下身形由敵右臂下攢過速
提右腿左掌向上穿再以右掌削擊其肋或以四指點戳
其肋而同時拗項回頭目視右掌

I quickly step my left foot and pull in my neck to
protect my head while dropping down and through
under his right arm. I quickly lift my right leg and
thread my left hand up then either slice [xiāo jī] his
ribs with my right hand, or stab [diǎn chuō] his ribs
with my four fingers together. While I do this, I turn
my head to look back at my right hand.

本招為甲乙丙丁戊五圖黑褲者即我灰褲者為敵請注意焉
Please take note that in each of the five drawings of this
exchange I am in black trousers and my opponent is in
grey trousers.

第二十七手名為巧破纏腰鎖

The twenty-seventh method is called Skillfully Break the Chains Coiled around the Waist [qiǎo pò chǎn yāo suǒ]

我與敵相較或又來第二者從身後將我抱住（又名玉帶纏腰）我速用全手指付按敵之全指以上再用指甲順其指甲根往回剝挖敵手必開

I am in an exchange with my opponent, or someone else comes up behind me to grab around my waist (this is called Jade Belt Around the Waist). I quickly press [àn] all my fingers along all his fingers, align my fingernails with the base of his fingernails, and dig under them to peel them back [bō wā]. My opponent must open his hands.

我速用左手扶右拳向後以肘打其胸此招之用法不一

I quickly strike his chest with my elbow, supporting
the strike by placing my left palm on my right fist. I
can continue on with a variety of techniques.

（一）速下腰由自襠下向後出手攀其腿至我臍腹敵
必傾倒

(One choice) I quickly drop my waist and thread my hands from under my groin towards my back in order to seize [pān] his legs and hold them to my belly. My opponent must fall over backwards.

（一）速提腿向後倒閃撩陰腿不遇仇敵萬勿用之

(Another choice) I quickly lift my leg and place it behind and slice up into my opponent's groin so that he can do nothing to counter my attack.

（一）如敵將我兩手及腰速同抱住我用漲力速下身
以兩手按自腿根而兩肘用力向外扭通身用合一勁漲
力敵手必開

(Another choice) If my opponent grabs my body and arms, I use swelling power [zhàng lì] and quickly drop my body down. I press my legs with both hands, then drive power into both elbows from my whole body to apply force outward with swelling power. My opponent must let go.

再向右轉身以左手扶右脈離咀相近如猴兒吃桃式同
時速掰落右步進其襠而虛之再通身用力以右臂撞其
肋同時右臂向外滾力右足再落實

I turn my body to the right and support my right wrist in my left hand near my mouth (like the position Monkey Eats a Peach). At the same time, I quickly take the weight off my right leg and open my right foot into my opponent's groin. I then use the force along my whole body to ram into [zhuàng] his ribs with my right arm. At the same time, I roll my right arm outward and put my weight onto my right leg.

本招為甲乙丙丁戊五圖黑褲者即我灰褲者為敵請注意焉
Please take note that in each of the five drawings of this exchange I am in black trousers and my opponent is in grey trousers.

第二十八手名為翻身羅漢掌

The twenty-eighth method is called Roll Over Arhat Palm [fān shēn luó hàn zhǎng]

敵來右手我速以右手扣其腕再同時用左掌由自肩上
發出探打其面

My opponent comes at me with his right hand. I quickly trap [kòu] his wrist with my right hand and at the same time reach out [tàn dǎ] over the shoulder to his face with my left hand.

敵必上封我左掌撤回

My opponent must close off my attack upwards
[shàng fēng], so I bring my left hand back.

THE TWENTY-EIGHTH METHOD

遂發右掌撞其胸敵封右手

I shove [zhuàng] his chest with my right hand, so he

shuts down [fēng] my right hand.

我速上起而急上扣左步落於敵之右腿傍同時速以左
掌正打其襠（不遇歹人萬不可用）

I quickly enter and advance my left foot, hooked in,
beside my opponent's right leg while at the same
time I quickly strike directly to his groin (don't use
this technique on someone who is not a vicious
enemy).

敵必卸我速向左轉身形起左掌再以右掌反打其襠如
遇他手隨機應變可也

My opponent must evade the attack. I quickly turn my body left, lift my left palm and strike again to his groin with my right palm turned over [fǎn dǎ]. If he gets a hand in to defend his groin, I need to change my technique according to the circumstances.

本招為甲乙丙丁戊五圖黑褲者即我灰褲者為敵請注
意焉 Please take note that in each of the five drawings of this exchange I am in black trousers and my opponent is in grey trousers.

第二十九手名為順水推舟

The twenty-ninth method is called Push a Boat Along with the Current [shùn shuǐ tuī zhōu]

敵以右拳擊我胸

My opponent punches at my chest with his right fist.

我速用右掌由敵右腕外往上穿

I quickly thread my right palm up [shàng chuān] outside his right wrist.

而擴其腕

And grab [lü] his wrist.

THE TWENTY-NINTH METHOD

敵必起我再以左手托敵之右肘而我右手同時順敵右
臂上向其脖項推去捏其咽喉同時上右步落於敵之右
步後

My opponent must lift (to get away), so I lift [tuō] his right elbow with my left hand and slide along on top of his right arm with my right hand to push towards his neck until I can grab [niē 'knead'] his throat. At the same time, I advance my right foot behind his right leg.

而進身形以一力擊之可也

I enter with the force of my whole body working together.

本招為甲乙丙丁戊五圖黑褲者即我灰褲者為敵請注意焉 Please take note that in each of the five drawings of this exchange I am in black trousers and my opponent is in grey trousers.

第三十手名為倒踢紫金冠

The thirtieth method is called Kick Over the Mourning Cap [dǎo tī zǐ jīn guān]

我用左掌擊敵之右肩敵用左手扣我左腕而用右手托我肘

I strike my opponent's right shoulder with my left palm. He grabs [kòu] my left wrist with his left hand and lifts my elbow with his right hand.

向左側扭身遂上右步我即被拿我當速扣左步向右扭
身遂提右腿

He twists his body left and steps the right foot
forward so that I am caught (ready for a joint lock). I
quickly hook my left foot in [kòu bù], twist my body
to the right and lift my right leg.

THE THIRTIETH METHOD

抬頭向上折腰挺項以右腿踢敵腹諸同志果如用此招
時或以前所有撩陰等招數若不遇匪人萬不可踢其襠
注重套德是好武者之本以公報私得手不容人乃匹夫
之也

I raise my head and neck and bend my back [zhé yāo] to kick my right leg up into his abdomen. Please note for this technique and previous techniques which attack the groin – do not under any circumstances kick anyone other than a real enemy in the groin. Respect for ethics is the root of a good martial artist. To brutalize someone to serve one's own ego – to keep hitting someone without giving face – is the mark of a ruffian.

本招為甲乙丙三圖黑褲者即我灰褲者為敵請注意焉
Please take note that in each of the three drawings of this exchange I am in black trousers and my opponent is in grey trousers.

第三十一手名為上步橫衝掌

The thirty-first method is called Advance to Charge Across [shàng bù héng chōng zhǎng]

敵以右掌擊我胸我速吸胸而卸之同時扭身形用右手
順敵臂外往下插

My opponent strikes at my chest with his right hand. I quickly suck in my chest to evade while twisting my body and sliding my right hand along the outer edge of his arm to stab downward [xià chā].

再向側衝其臂而化其力再吞右手同時上左步而虛之

I then charge into [chōng] his arm to disrupt his force and control his right hand. At the same time, I step my left foot in with the weight off it.

待敵力解必抽右手我遂坐身形鬆肩墜肘腰間用力以
雙掌擊其右肋可也

I wait until his force dissipates [lì jiě] and he must
bring his right hand back. I settle down, release my
shoulders and drop my elbows to hit his right ribs
with both palms – using the full force of my body
core.

本招為甲乙丙三圖黑褲者即我灰褲者為敵請注意焉
Please take note that in each of the three drawings of
this exchange I am in black trousers and my
opponent is in grey trousers.

第三十二手名為順手牽羊

The thirty-second method is called Lead the Sheep Along at Your Ease [shùn shǒu qiàn yáng]

敵向我面撲擊來我速用右手由其臂外穿去

My opponent pounces [pū jī] towards my face. I quickly thread my right hand out along the outer edge of his arm.

復攄其腕同時虛右步以左手附兜其肘借敵之撲力而
向右側領帶之

I pull his wrist while I take my weight off my right leg and cup his elbow with my left hand. I use his pouncing forward energy to lead [lǐng dài] him to my right side.

同時遂出右腿使足橫其膝敵必敗

As I pull, I simultaneously put out my right foot and
sweep it across [héng] his knee, and he must lose this
exchange.

本招為甲乙丙三圖黑褲者即我灰褲者為敵請注意焉
Please take note that in each of the three drawings of
this exchange I am in black trousers and my
opponent is in grey trousers.

第三十三手名為蛇形掌

The thirty-third method is called Snake Form [shé xíng zhǎng]

敵以右掌擊我胸我速吸身而虛右步用右手順其臂外
由上往下吃而纏其臂至我臂在敵臂下時速將右不落
實塌肩坐身以右掌手心朝下四指戳其肋腋

My opponent strikes to my chest with his right hand. I quickly absorb with my body and take my weight off my right leg while sliding my right hand along the outer edge of his arm and coiling [chǎn] it under from above to control his arm. When my arm arrives under his arm I quickly move forward onto my right leg, settle my shoulder and settle my body down. With my right palm facing down, I poke to his armpit with my four fingers.

敵必掛卸之我速上扣左步同時再以左掌心朝上順其
右臂上發出點其目

My opponent must evade my attack. I quickly enter with my left foot hooked in [kòu bù] while at the same time I turn my left palm up and slide it along above his right arm to dab [diǎn] his eye.

敵必上封我速將右手撤回提起右腿向右轉身形而右
掌再由我右肩上發出戳其目同時扭項折腰看敵面

My opponent must close off the upper attack [shàng

fēng], so I quickly bring my right hand back and lift

my right leg. I turn my body to the right and shoot my

right hand out again, over my right shoulder, to poke

[chuō] his eye. While I do this, I turn my neck and

bend back to look at his face.

敵必托我肘我速落右步而反右腕仍戳其目

My opponent must lift my elbow. When he does this, I quickly land my right foot and turn my right wrist over to poke [chuō] his eye yet again.

敵必仍托我肘卸之我再上扣左步向上穿左掌再以右
掌擊其左肋是招所用之法即此如敵變招我隨機鷹變
而已矣

My opponent must lift my elbow again to dissipate
my attack. I enter my left foot hooked in again and
thread [shàng chuān] my left hand up while I hit his
ribs with my right palm. This technique practises
changing tactics as my opponent changes
techniques.

本招為甲乙丙丁戊五圖黑褲者即我灰褲者為敵請注
意焉 Please take note that in each of the seven
drawings of this exchange I am in black trousers and
my opponent is in grey trousers.

第三十四手名為前鏨腿

The thirty-fourth method is called Chisel in with the Leg [qián zàn tuǐ]

敵來左手我以左手擄之

My opponent comes at me with his left hand, so I pull [lǚ] it with my left hand.

敵必撤我亦撤手而同時起右腿順我左臂下平伸以足
尖點其左肋須向後折腰重量載於左腿如鐵板橋式相
仿是所謂也

My opponent must step back. I move my hand and lift my right leg and stretch it straight out under my left arm to poke the toes [diǎn] into his left ribs. I must lean back and plant my weight into my left leg. My position is like an iron bridge.

本招為甲乙二圖黑褲者即我灰褲者為敵請注意焉
Please take note that in each of the two drawings of this exchange I am in black trousers and my opponent is in grey trousers.

PRONUNCIATION OF PINYIN, THE CHINESE NATIONAL PHONETIC ALPHABET (WITH INTERNATIONAL PHONETIC ALPHABET EQUIVALENTS)

INITIALS (words can start with these consonants, or have a zero initial)		
PINYIN	IPA	ROUGH PRONUNCIATION GUIDE
p	p^h	Like English pet with a considerable puff of air.
b	p	Similar to the *pinyin* "p" but without the puff of air (unvoiced, neither English pet nor bet).
t	t^h	Like English tag with a considerable puff of air.
d	t	Similar to the *pinyin* "t" but with no puff of air (unvoiced, not dog).
k	k^h	Like English kill with a considerable puff of air.
g	k	Similar to the *pinyin* "k" but with no puff of air (unvoiced, not English get).
c	ts^h	Like exaggerating English cats.
z	ts	Like the *pinyin* "c" but without the puff of air (unvoiced).
ch	$tʂ^h$	Somewhat similar to English chat with a puff of air, but with the tip of the tongue rolled back.
zh	tʂ	Like the *pinyin* "ch" but with no puff of air (unvoiced).
q	$tɕ^h$	Somewhat similar to English chat with a puff of air, but with the front of the tongue raised and the tip on the lower teeth.
j	tɕ	Like the *pinyin* "q" but without the puff of air (unvoiced).
m	m	Like English met.
n	n	Like English net.
f	f	Similar to English fat, but with the teeth just touching lightly behind the lower lip.

s	s	Similar to English <u>s</u>et.
sh	ṣ	Somewhat similar to English <u>sh</u>ow, but with the same tongue placement as the *pinyin* "ch" and "zh."
x	þ	Somewhat similar to English <u>sh</u>ine but with the same tongue placement as the *pinyin* "q" and "j."
h	χ	Raise the back of the tongue and let the breath come through the obstructed passage without vibrating the vocal cords.
l	l	Like English <u>l</u>et.
r	ɹ	Like the *pinyin* "sh" but with voicing.

FINALS

n	n	Like English pi<u>n</u>.
ng	ŋ	Like English si<u>ng</u>.

VOWELS

a	A a ɛ	Usually close to English f<u>a</u>ther (not p<u>a</u>t). Like y<u>e</u>t when written "-ian" or "yan."
e	ɣ e ɛ ə	Usually similar to English p<u>e</u>t, can tend towards a mid vowel.
i	i ɭ ɪ	Usually similar to English b<u>ee</u>. Similar to w<u>e</u>t when written "ui." After c, z, s, ch, zh, sh, and r it is similar to s<u>ir</u>.
o	o u	Usually close to English r<u>o</u>ll. Similar to c<u>ow</u> when written "ao," and <u>owe</u> when in "ou."
u	u y	Usually similar t English o b<u>oo</u>t. After the *pinyin* "x", "q", and "j" and in the vowel groups starting with these consonants, it is pronounced "ü".
ü	y	Similar to French <u>ü</u>. It is written after "n" or "l," because these are the only positions where both "u" and "ü" are possible
y	i	Partially like an English 'y', tending towards i.

w	u	Partially like an English 'w', tending towards u.

TONES IN PINYIN			
NUMBER	PINYIN	NAME	RANGE
1	ˉ	high level	55
2	´	high rising	35
3	ˇ	dipping	214
4	`	high falling	51
none	° or blank	neutral	in context

With tone sandhi, tones may change according to the preceding or following tone.

The tone marking is put over the main vowel when there are two vowels written together (usually involving the pronunciation of y or w).

About the translator

Andrea Falk has practised external and internal Chinese martial arts since 1972. She has studied Chinese and Japanese art, geography, history, language, literature, philosophy, politics, religion, and sociology since then, as well. She received a Bachelor of Arts majoring in Chinese (1978), a Bachelor of Physical Education (1980) and a Master of Physical Education with an emphasis on coaching science (1991) from the University of British Columbia. She trained wushu full time on a scholarship from 1980 to 1983 at the Beijing Physical Culture Institute, earning an advanced studies diploma in wushu under the tutelage of professor Xia Bohua. There she learned the basics of Yang and Chen style Taijiquan, Baguazhang, Xingyiquan, Chaquan, Tongbeiquan, and modern Wushu (Changquan and weapons).

From 1984 she continued her studies in only the internal styles (counting Aikido as an internal style), and purely traditionally, visiting China on extended trips as often as possible. Her training includes Chen style Taijiquan, Jiang style Baguazhang, and Jiang Rongqiao's Taiji Changquan in Shanghai, Xingyiquan and the Cheng, Liang, and Ma Gui styles of Baguazhang in Beijing.

Andrea has taught the Chinese martial arts professionally since graduation in 1983. She travels twice a year to teach ongoing groups around Canada and England. For many years Andrea translated materials for her students, and in 2000 established tgl books to bring Chinese martial arts books to a wider audience.

Yan Dehua's
Bagua
Applications

閻德華的八卦掌使用法

tgl books

trois   gros   lapins   traversent   le   chemin

ISBN 978-1-989468-23-4

9 781989 468234 >